Queen Victoria ruled Britain from 1837 to 1901. Many of the grand buildings in Britain, such as shops and banks, bridges and railway stations, were built in Victorian times. Photography was one of the Victorians' many inventions, along with the railways.

a Victorian railway station

Britain was a rich and powerful nation under Queen Victoria. The **Industrial Revolution** was changing people's lives as well as their cities and towns. Mills, mines and factories were making **mass-produced** goods for the first time and the railways meant that goods as well as people could travel faster than before.

But although many people were becoming rich, others lived in terrible **poverty**. Families were much bigger than they are today, often with ten children or more. In early Victorian times, there was no free schooling and life for many children was hard as they had to work to earn money to take home. Many had to start work as early as four years old, down dark and dingy coal mines or in noisy cotton mills and factories, where they worked up to 16 hours a day. Children had few **legal rights** and they were often badly treated by their masters, who punished them by beating them or throwing them into cold water. It sounds like a nightmare today, but for many children this was just how life was.

This book will tell you more about the lives of Victorian children and about the terrible jobs many of them had to do.

FACT

Queen Victoria was queen of Britain and the British **Empire**, which included many countries such as India, Canada and Australia. She ruled over a quarter of the world's population.

HARD TIMES

Growing up in the Victorian Age

Jillian Powell

⁕ Contents ⁕

Collins

⇝ The Victorians ⇜

Children in Victorian times lived very different lives from yours today. In many ways, they were treated like little adults. Unless they came from a rich family, they had to go out to work to earn money. But it was not work like today's holiday jobs or paper rounds. It meant working long hours six days a week, doing horrible jobs that were boring or dangerous, or both!

children in Victorian days

⇝ Home life ⇜

The Victorians didn't have many of the home comforts you enjoy today. There was no radio or television and few machines to make life easier, so jobs like washing dishes and clothes had to be done by hand. Most houses didn't have running water or bathrooms. They usually had an outdoor toilet called a privy.

In richer households, maids had to carry water from the kitchen to fill baths or washing bowls. All the cooking and hot water came from a range oven in the kitchen, which was heated by coal. Their houses would feel very cold to you, as they had no central heating and the only warmth came from coal or wood fires. They would also seem dark, as there was no electric lighting and rooms were lit by gloomy gas lamps downstairs and oil lamps or candles upstairs.

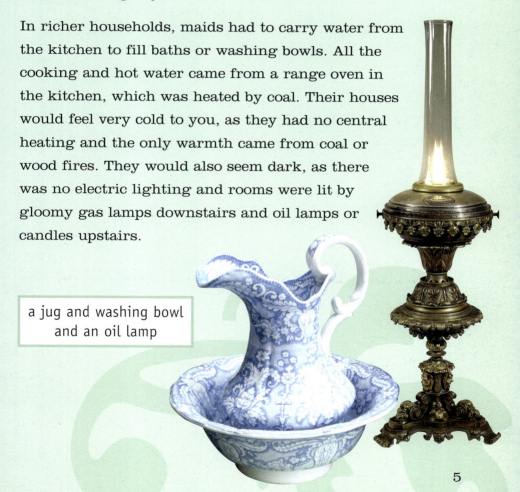

a jug and washing bowl and an oil lamp

The Victorians liked dark furniture and wallpaper in strong colours like red, brown and green. They filled their rooms with ornaments, collections of shells or birds' eggs, plants and other belongings. Dining tables were usually covered with a heavy dark cloth.

a wealthy Victorian's living room

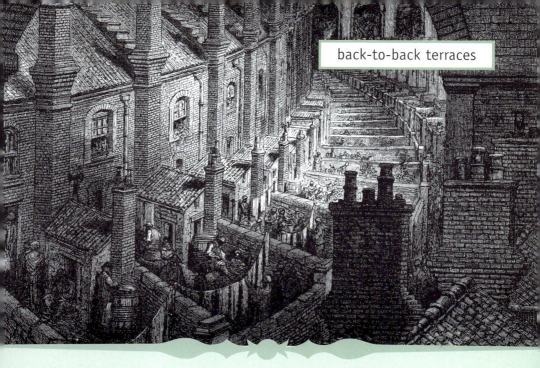

back-to-back terraces

Poor families lived in small, crowded houses built in back-to-back rows. Many had only two rooms. They were dirty and dark inside, as the windows were often broken and stuffed with rags to keep out the cold. Often children had to share a room, and even a bed, with their parents.

The poorest children lived in orphanages or cheap lodging houses, with up to 30 sharing a room and sleeping on rough rag or straw beds. Some children were even forced to sleep on the streets if they had not earned enough in the day to pay for lodgings.

FACT
The Public Health Act of 1848 brought in laws for clean water and **sewerage** services.

⇒ Going to school ⇐

In early Victorian times, most children did not go to school. There were no free state schools as there are today. There were only church or charity schools, or dame schools run by old women in their homes. Rich children usually had a tutor or **governess** to teach them at home and boys sometimes went on to a private day or boarding school. Some poor children were sent to ragged schools, which gave them food and lodgings as well as lessons, but many had no schooling as they had to work to bring in money for the family. After 1870, local School Boards were set up to open a school in every town and village.

children at a dame school

The bright classroom displays, computers and libraries in your schools are very different from the bare, stark classrooms of Victorian schools. They were dimly lit by gas lights and the only heating was a smoky stove in the corner.

It was sometimes so cold in winter that the inkwells in the desks froze over. Boys and girls often went in by separate doors and sat in rows of wooden desks all facing the teacher at the front. Most girls wore **pinafores** over their dresses and boys wore caps, trousers and jackets.

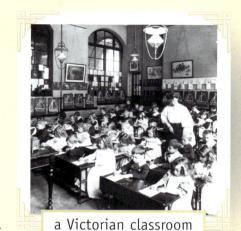

a Victorian classroom

The only other classroom equipment was some books, an **abacus** for mathematics and a globe for geography. On the walls there might be a map and a picture of Queen Victoria. Children spent most of the day copying from the blackboard. The main subjects were reading, writing, arithmetic and religious instruction. Children wrote in chalk on slate boards that they could wipe clean and use again. The teacher used a whistle and a cane to keep strict discipline, punishing pupils by caning them or making them stand in the corner for hours wearing a pointed dunce's cap.

at school

FACT
In 1891 the Government made schooling free and compulsory for all children.

✦ Entertainment and toys ✦

Think what part technology plays in your free time and entertainment – MP3 players, computers, games consoles and mobile phones. Victorian children had none of these. The music they heard came mainly from singers or bands, and sometimes street buskers and organ-grinders, who played the same few tunes all the time and kept people entertained with a monkey trained to collect money from the crowd. There were street entertainments too, like acrobats, clowns and dancing bears.

an organ-grinder

Poor children had few toys and little free time, with only Sunday off work. Children played outdoors a lot, making up songs and chants, or playing skipping, chasing or hopping games in the street.

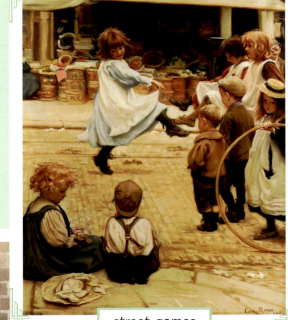

street games

playing with a hoop

Most children only had simple toys like hoops, whipping tops, stilts, skipping ropes and balls. They could buy pencils, beads and badges for a penny each from cheap shops called Penny Bazaars.

DID YOU KNOW?
In Victorian money, there were 12 pennies to a shilling and 20 shillings to a pound.

Richer children had toys like dolls, teddy bears, toy soldiers, jack-in-the-boxes, clockwork toys, railways and toy theatres. They often kept scrapbooks and collected shells, stamps and even birds' eggs (which is illegal today).

Nowadays, computers and televisions mean that everyone in a family may be doing something different in their free time. But the Victorians thought that doing things as a family was very important. In the evening, the whole family joined in, playing new card games like **happy families** or board games like **ludo**, or singing songs around the piano.

Children from rich families had many toys.

❧ Clothes ❧

Getting dressed would have taken a lot longer in Victorian times. There were no zips, elastic or Velcro fastenings. Clothes had to be buttoned or laced, and even boots and shoes had buttonhooks to fasten. Children were dressed like little grown-ups, wearing lots of different garments, from hats and gloves, to vests and petticoats.

Today you can wear light, easy-care fabrics designed for every kind of sport and weather, but in Victorian times clothes were made in natural fabrics like wool, linen and cotton. Washing the clothes took a whole day each week, as they had to be hand-washed, or a turn-handle washing machine might be used, then irons had to be heated up on the fire to press every garment and frill.

an old-fashioned iron

Richer children had clothes that followed the fashions of the day. Boys wore dresses until they were about five, then long trousers with jackets, waistcoats, shirts and bows or **stocks**. Girls wore dresses and aprons and several layers of underwear including frilled trousers called pantalettes, petticoats and white stockings. Rich boys might be dressed in sailor suits or velvet knickerbocker suits, which consisted of breeches, tight jackets and frilled shirts. Queen Victoria's love for Scotland set off a trend for tartan trousers and kilts.

Victorian boys' clothes

Poor children had little money for clothes or fashions. Many wore rags tied or held together with pins and went barefoot because they could not afford to buy shoes or boots. Often their clothes were dirty and torn from the work they had to do.

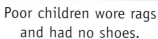

Poor children wore rags and had no shoes.

15

Victorian towns and cities may not have had today's cars, but the streets were crowded and noisy with horse-drawn cabs and buses, and with people trying to make a living. In London, many children began working as street sellers at the age of seven. They worked long days, often starting at 4 o'clock in the morning and working until 9 or 10 o'clock at night. Some helped the costermongers, who sold fruit and vegetables from stalls or barrows. Others went to the markets at dawn to buy stock, then sold it from baskets in the street. Some were flower girls and went from house to house trying to sell their **posies**, or sold them to passers-by in the street. Many stood barefoot, because they had no shoes, shouting out to try to sell their goods.

a flower-seller

DID YOU KNOW?
The costermongers invented their own secret language. Sometimes they spoke words backwards – for example, *reeb* meant beer.

Some boys, called bootblacks, worked all day polishing the boots and shoes of people who stopped to pay them. They were often boys from ragged homes, trying to earn a few pennies.

Other children earned money by singing songs, busking or tumbling. The street tumblers ran beside cabs and buses, doing cartwheels and somersaults. Some worked for masters who trained them to do tricks, sometimes even tying up their arms and legs to make them bend more!

a family of street tumblers

As there were no telephones in Victorian times, many children could earn a few pennies carrying messages. Messenger boys had to stand all day on boxes in the street, waiting for people to give them messages to carry. Others carried parcels or opened cab doors for rich people. Some boys were paid to run **errands** for shopkeepers.

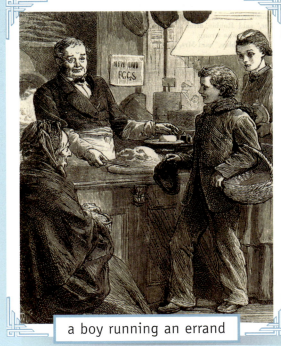

a boy running an errand

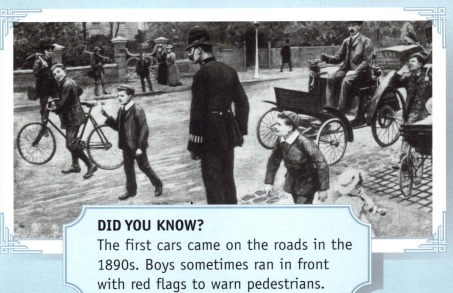

DID YOU KNOW?
The first cars came on the roads in the 1890s. Boys sometimes ran in front with red flags to warn pedestrians.

Imagine the smell and muck on city streets busy with horse-drawn cabs, buses and carts. Cleaning up all the horse manure was the job of the crossing sweepers and orderly boys. The crossing sweepers would dodge between the carriages with their brooms, sweeping the roads clean for passers-by. The long skirts of Victorian dresses could become filthy in the dust and dirt of the streets.

a crossing sweeper

Orderly boys had the job of shovelling up all the horse muck and putting it into bins. They wore red clothes so that they could be seen easily in the busy road traffic. Others worked as "pure" collectors. Their job was to clean up all the dog mess from the streets.

You might enjoy **beachcombing** when you go to the seaside, but how about wading up to your knees in a muddy river all day, hunting for bits of scrap you could sell? This was how many poor children who lived near the River Thames in London spent their days. The river was busy with coal barges and other ships. It was very polluted with sewage and chemicals.

the River Thames in Victorian times

It was in these murky waters that boys and girls aged between eight and 14 years worked as mudlarks or "river finders". When the tide was low, they waded out barefoot into the river, hunting for anything they could sell, such as bits of coal, copper nails, rope or bones. They could sell a pot of coal to poor families living nearby, or take rope, bones and nails to a Rag Shop. Most earned about three pennies a day.

It was cold, dirty work standing all day in the mud and pollution of a busy river. Children often stood in the wastewater from steam-powered factories to warm up their frozen feet. They got cuts and grazes from broken glass and nails on the riverbed. Sometimes they had a lucky find such as an old saw or hammer that had fallen from one of the ships in dock for repair. They often worked in groups of 20 or 30, using baskets, old kettles and hats to collect their findings. Some were caught and put in prison for stealing coal from the river barges.

a mudlark

❧ In the mines ❧

The Victorians needed coal to power their factories, steam ships and trains, as well as for cooking and heating. Mine owners had new machines for digging deeper underground. From the mineshaft, a network of narrow tunnels ran for many miles underground. Some of these tunnels were too small for ponies to work in, so children were used instead.

Imagine having to crawl in total darkness, through narrow underground tunnels dripping with water. You might only see the sun once a week on your day off, spending all other daylight hours underground. You would be in danger too, due to the constant risk of explosion from coal gas, or of getting trapped if a tunnel were to fall in.

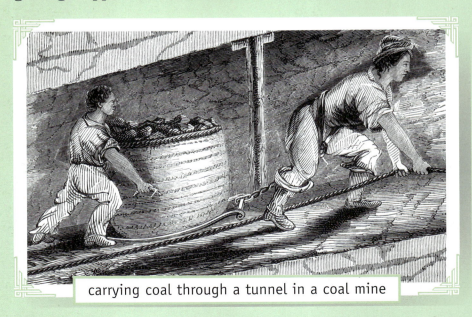

carrying coal through a tunnel in a coal mine

This is how life was for children sent to work as hurriers in the coal mines. They had to push or pull the coal carts through the tunnels, hauling them along by chains fixed to their belts. They were mostly working on their hands and knees scrambling through tunnels that were less than half their height.

working the winding gear

The hurriers were also at risk from falling coal and cave-ins. Children were often in charge of the winding gear that raised and lowered workers into the pit shaft. Many died in accidental falls and those who survived were often bullied and beaten by the miners.

opening a door to let the coal cart through

Children also worked as trappers, which meant they had to open the doors in the mines to let the coal carts through. They began work at 4 o'clock in the morning and didn't come out until half past five in the afternoon. Mostly they sat in the dark, waiting for the rattling sound of the carts approaching. Candles or lamps could be dangerous, so their eyes must have grown used to long hours of total blackness. Sometimes, rats would steal the bread or cheese they had taken in to eat. Trappers were not allowed to leave their post, because if the doors were not opened dangerous gases could build up in the tunnels, but some children still died in explosions.

FACT
In 1842 the Government banned all females and boys under ten from working underground.

Most children started work in coal mines at the age of eight or nine. Some worked the pumps to keep water out of the tunnels and they often had to stand with their feet in cold water for eight hours a day. In Scotland, girls had to carry baskets of coal up the ladders beside the pit shafts, even though their loads could weigh up to 150 kilograms.

135cm

120cm

DID YOU KNOW?
Today, the average ten-year-old is 135 centimetres tall. In 1836, the average height for a child of that age was 121 centimetres. However, this still meant that children had to crawl, as some tunnels were less than 50 centimetres high.

⤞ In the metalworks ⤝

Even for those working above ground, mines and metal works were nasty and dangerous places. Washer boys had the job of washing the **lead ore** that their fathers had dug out of the lead mines. The Victorians used lead for plumbing and roofs, and it was even an ingredient in paints, cosmetics and bread! (Today we know that lead is poisonous and by the 1980s, very little lead was still used in making things.)

The washer boys had to smash up the lead ore with hammers first, then load it by hand into a sieve on a long handle. They then had to pump the sieve up and down into a tub of cold water. It must have been backbreaking work and they often caught colds or were cut by flying fragments of iron ore.

sieving lead ore

Most worked 12-hour days from 7 o'clock in the morning to 7 o'clock at night, with an hour's break for lunch. They were paid four pennies a day.

Iron, tin and copper were used in building and manufacturing. In the metalworks, boys worked in unbearable heat. They often breathed in sulphurous fumes that made them cough and stunted their growth. Some boys had to work 24-hour **shifts**, stoking up the furnaces with coal. Their skin could get burnt by hot, runny metal and some even lost arms when they got trapped in the machinery.

beating metal in the metalworks

⇒ In the mills and factories ⇐

Victorian mills and factories were big, noisy places with huge clanking machines powered by steam. The machinery and gas lighting made them hot and uncomfortable places to work. Many children had to start work at half past five in the morning and work until 8 o'clock at night. Sometimes their masters would alter the clocks in order to make them work longer, but they were too afraid of punishment to complain.

sweeping up fluff in a textile mill

Cotton was imported and made into **textiles** in huge cotton mills. The air was full of fluff that gave the children **asthma** and some even became trapped or crushed in moving machinery.

The youngest children worked as scavengers. They had to crawl under the **spinning mules** that spun the cotton thread and brush up any pieces of cotton fluff. The fluff had to be cleared away constantly to avoid the risk of fire.

Piecers had to piece together any threads that broke while the machine was working. They had to stand all day, walking around the spinning mule to watch for broken threads. When a thread broke, they spat on the ends and twisted them together. Children began working as piecers at the age of six. Sometimes they were so small that they had to wear blocks on their shoes in order to reach the machines.

FACT

Mill and factory owners employed child workers because they could squeeze into small spaces between machinery. They could also pay them less than adults.

a piecer mending broken thread

Children were also employed to do jobs in potteries and brickworks. These were hot and dusty places to work and the air was full of clay dust and poisonous lead glaze. Some children worked as jigger turners, which meant they had to stand all day turning the handle of the potter's wheel. Others had to mould the handles for teacups, pressing down the moulds one after another with their chests.

Boys aged between six and ten worked as mould carriers. They had to carry heavy plate moulds full of clay from the potter's wheel to the furnaces. This meant running up to seven miles a day and often working up to 16 hours a day for **half a crown** a week. Sometimes they were sent out to run errands, going from the heat of the furnaces into the cold outdoors. Many died from **tuberculosis** or asthma attacks.

mass-production of plates in a pottery

In the brick factories, children worked as clay carriers. They had to run backwards and forwards carrying lumps of wet clay on their heads to the brick-maker's bench. Their necks must have ached at the end of the day, as each load could weigh up to 20 kilograms.

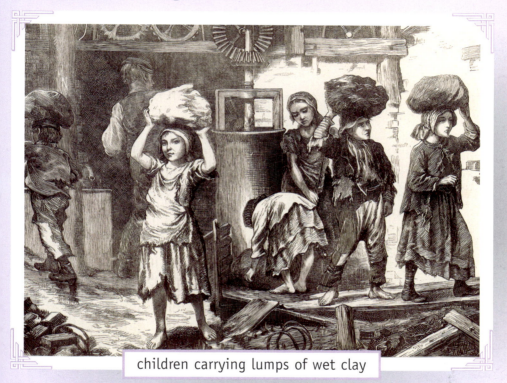

children carrying lumps of wet clay

In the flour mills, girls worked as damsels. Their job was to load grain onto the mill wheel. They had to work fast because of the danger of sparks flying off an empty mill wheel. There was so much flour dust in the air that there was always a risk of explosions.

Many girls worked in match factories, dipping matchsticks into **phosphorus** all day. The fumes from the chemical were poisonous and over time they caused a disease called "phossy jaw", which ate away at the girls' jawbones.

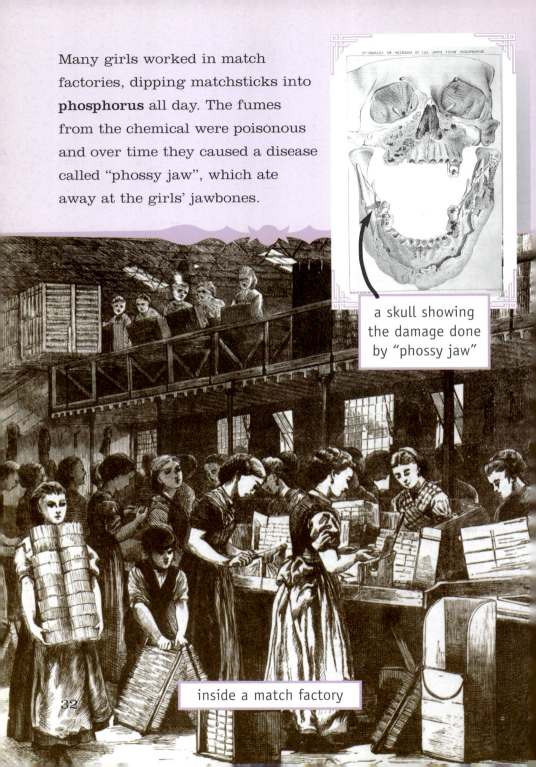

a skull showing the damage done by "phossy jaw"

inside a match factory

Sheffield, in Yorkshire, had a busy industry of cutlery factories. Children worked on the grinding wheels, making knives, forks and spoons. They breathed in metal dust, which made them cough and gave them lung diseases.

Nail-making workshops took children from the age of seven. One child had the job of working the bellows to keep the fire going. Others stood at the benches hammering out hundreds of nails every day. Boys would also work the bellows in a **blacksmith's** forge.

FACT
The 1833 Factory Act banned children under nine from working in textile mills. It limited the working day to eight hours for nine- to 13-year-olds.

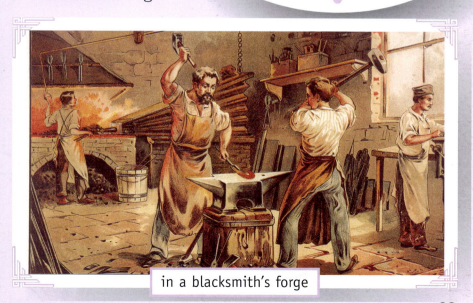

in a blacksmith's forge

❧ In houses ❧

Today, open fires are a luxury that we may enjoy as well as central heating, but in Victorian times all houses and offices were heated by coal fires. The chimneys needed sweeping every year, but the sweeps didn't have the powerful vacuum cleaners and brushes that they do today. They had climbing boys instead. They were boys as young as four years old who were forced to climb up inside chimneys to clean out the soot. They climbed using their knees, elbows and feet, carrying a brush and scraper to remove the soot. Some chimneys would still be hot from fires and measured as little as 18 centimetres across.

a climbing boy

Older children sometimes climbed behind the "chummy boys". They stuck pins in their feet or used burning straw to keep them moving. The children got soot in their eyes and their skin was often cut and grazed, but their masters just rubbed salty water into the cuts to harden them up. Some masters beat the boys with ropes to punish them.

Climbing boys worked for up to 16 hours a day and were paid only in food, mostly fatty meat and soups. Many slept in old soot bags and only had a bath once every few months. Some died from burns or because they got stuck in bends in the chimneys.

Chimney sweeping was often dangerous work.

For many girls, the most likely place to find work was in **domestic service**. Big houses had lots of servants, including **scullery** maids, lady's maids and kitchen maids. Most girls found a place when they were 12 or 13 years old and worked as "tweenies", helping other servants, or as "slaveys", who were maids of all work. They had to get up at 5 o'clock in the morning, clean, dust, carry up water, help the cook, then clean the fire grates and run errands.

plucking a chicken for dinner

They worked very long hours for low wages of only £3 or £4 a year, but work in a household meant they had lodgings and clothes to wear. Some girls went in as day maids, working from 8 o'clock in the morning to 8 o'clock at night. Many girls who lived in charity homes were sent out to houses as steppers. Their job was to brush and wash the doorstep, for which they were paid a penny a time.

Children were also employed in big houses to do odd jobs or run errands. Boys worked as pages or footboys, beginning work at the age of eight. They worked long days from 6 o'clock in the morning to 8 o'clock at night. They had to do jobs like emptying the ash from the fireplaces every morning, cleaning windows, or washing and polishing all the knives and silver.

Lamp boys had the job of checking all the candles and lamps. Large houses would have a huge collection of oil lamps. The lamp boy had to fill them with oil, trim the wicks and clean the lamps. Hall boys or bootboys had to clean all the boots and shoes for the family, the servants and even house guests.

The lamp boy finishes at last.

❧ On the land ❧

Today, most farm jobs can be carried out by big machinery.
Work which once took teams of people several days to finish
can now be done in a single day. In Victorian times, many
jobs were still done by hand, although steam-powered
machines began to be used on bigger farms. It was backbreaking work in the fields, whatever the weather. Some
children were paid to watch over sheep, making sure they
did not stray. Others worked as
human scarecrows, running up
and down the fields with wooden
clappers to keep the birds off
the newly planted seed. They worked
for just four pennies a day.

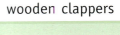

wooden clappers

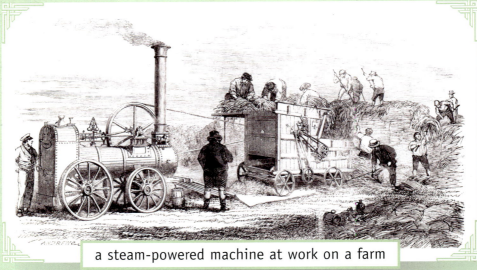

a steam-powered machine at work on a farm

The new steam-powered machines were noisy monsters, which many people saw as a threat because they were taking their jobs away. Threshing machines did the job of separating the grain from the rough outer **chaff**. Chaff boys had to stand all day in clouds of chaff and dust beside the machine, bagging up the chaff as it poured out.

Children as young as four were taught to plait straw to make hats and bonnets. They sat outdoors, using their own spit to make the straw damp and easier to work.

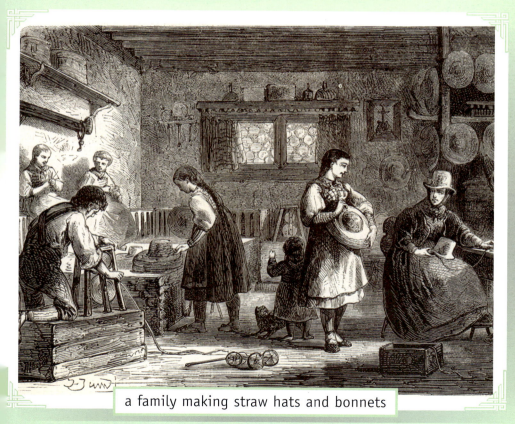

a family making straw hats and bonnets

You might go to school by car or bus, or perhaps it's a short walk from home. For many children in Victorian times, the day began with a walk of several miles to reach the farm. On bigger farms, children worked with women in farm gangs. A gang master who was in charge of the work rounded them up each morning, then many spent 14-hour days out in the field. They had to do jobs like **hoeing** and weeding, spreading **manure** or picking up stones from the ground.

children off to work on a farm

Fruit picking, harvest time and haymaking were the busiest times for farm gangs. In winter, many children worked as turnip pickers. It was hard work as the ground was often frozen because of frost or snow. Children who worked in farm gangs were often punished with a beating by the gang master for talking or resting.

After the crops had been harvested, children helped the women to "glean" for bits of grain. They had to walk up and down the fields, searching for any grain left behind from the harvest. They worked all the hours of daylight to find enough grain to make into flour for bread.

girls gleaning for grain

☙ Changes for the better ❧

Your life would have been very different if you had been born in Victorian times. At the beginning of the Victorian period, there were few laws protecting children, which is why many lived in terrible poverty and had to work long hours, often in dangerous conditions. Their masters could order them about and punish them just for falling asleep or talking during work.

The poorest people ended up in workhouses, which gave basic food and lodging in return for long hours of work. But slowly things began to change as people became more aware of what was going on and some Members of Parliament and journalists began to **campaign** for children's rights.

boys in the workhouse

Henry Mayhew, who wrote about the poor in London

The journalist Henry Mayhew (1812–1887) began to write newspaper articles about the lives of poor people working in London. He interviewed hundreds of people, including children, about their lives and published his work *London Labour and the London Poor* in 1865. Charles Booth (1840–1916) was another writer who investigated what life was like for poor people in the city, and he worked with a team of researchers that included his cousin, the writer Beatrix Potter (1866–1943). People living in Britain were shocked to read these reports and they began to call for the Government to do more to protect children and to help people living in poverty.

Lord Shaftesbury, who campaigned to help the poor

A number of Members of Parliament and Lords began to campaign for changes to the laws on children working in mines and factories. The Earl of Shaftesbury (1801–1885) became a **champion** of children's rights, bringing three important Factory Acts through Parliament, as well as the Coal Mines Act, which prevented all females and boys under the age of 13 from working underground. Lord Shaftesbury was also one of the founders of the Ragged Schools Union, which was set up because there were not enough dame, church or charity schools to educate all the children in need. By 1850, the Union had set up more than 100 schools for poor children, many offering food and shelter as well as lessons in reading, writing and arithmetic.

Another important champion for children was Dr Thomas Barnardo (1845–1905). He set up his own ragged school in London, then began to open homes giving shelter for homeless children. He found and rescued children living rough on the streets and provided them with shelter, clothes and food in the homes that he set up. He also established schemes for foster parents to take in homeless children, sending visitors to inspect the homes to make sure that the children would be properly cared for.

girls at work in the ironing room of a Barnardo's home

More homes were opened by the Children's Society, which was founded by Edward Rudolf in 1881. His cottage homes housed up to ten children between the ages of five and 14, with a master and matron acting as their carers.

FACT

Dr Thomas Barnardo set up his first children's home in 1870.

❧ Children and work today ❧

Nowadays, there are many more laws protecting children than there were in Victorian times. Children's basic freedoms and rights from birth are set out in the United Nations Convention on the Rights of the Child of 1989. Many countries have also made their own laws stating children's rights and protecting them from harm and abuse. But around the world millions of children still live in poverty and have no proper schooling because they are sent out to work to bring in money for their families. Others are sent to fight in wars, or are cruelly treated by their parents or masters.

a child scavenging on a rubbish dump

One in six children, or around 246 million worldwide, are forced into child labour. Most work in Asia and the Pacific region and 171 million are working in dangerous conditions such as down mines, or with chemicals and pesticides or dangerous machinery. In sub-Saharan Africa, one in three children under 15 years old is made to work.

This boy has collected any scrap of value, like metal cans.

Over two-thirds of all working children work on the land and do jobs like fetching water, fuel or food for animals. Millions more are employed for long hours for very low wages in workshops making clothes and other goods. Girls are often made to serve as maids in the houses of richer families, or as unpaid help in their own family.

Many children lack basics like clean clothing.

So in some parts of the world, child labour is just as real today as it was in Victorian Britain. But organisations like **UNICEF** and Christian Aid are working to put a stop to it and to protect children's rights. You can help by learning about their work and supporting their campaigns. You can also try to find out where the things you buy are made and check that the companies that make them do not use child labour. We can all help to fight for children's rights around the world, as people once did in Victorian Britain.

a school in Africa

✥ Glossary ✥

abacus
a simple counting device using beads on rows

asthma
a condition that can make breathing difficult

beachcombing
searching a beach for anything washed up by the sea

blacksmith
someone who works iron with a furnace, anvil and hammer

campaign
a course of action to try to change something

chaff
the tough outer skin of a seed

champion
a person who fights for the rights of others

domestic service
employment in another person's house

Empire
lands under the rule of a single nation

errands
short trips undertaken to perform small jobs or to give messages

governess
a woman teacher employed in a private household

half a crown a coin that was worth two shillings and sixpence in pounds, shillings and pence before British currency became decimal

happy families a card game which involves trying to collect sets of families

hoeing breaking up the earth or weeding with a long-handled tool called a hoe

Industrial Revolution the rapid growth of industry in Britain from the late 1700s throughout the 1800s because of inventions including steam-powered machinery

lead ore rock from which lead can be extracted

legal rights benefits that you are entitled to by law

ludo a board game which involves moving counters around a board according to the throws of a die

manure animal waste used to fertilise farmland

mass-produced made in large numbers by machines

phosphorus	a poisonous chemical that easily catches fire
pinafore	a dress with a sleeveless top, worn over a blouse or jumper
posies	small bunches of flowers
poverty	the state of being poor and in need
scullery	a small room in which dirty kitchen work was done
sewerage	a system of pipes and drains to take away toilet waste from buildings
shifts	periods of time for doing work either by day or night
spinning mules	machines that spun cotton thread
stocks	ties worn round the neck
textiles	cloth made by weaving or knitting
tuberculosis	an infectious disease, common in Victorian times, that attacks the lungs
UNICEF	the United Nation's Children's Fund

Index

1833   The Factory Act bans children under nine from working in textile mills.

1842   The Coal Mines Act bans all females and boys under ten from working underground.

1844   The Ragged Schools Union is formed.

1844   The Factory Act limits working hours for children aged between nine and 13 to six hours a day.

1848   The Public Health Act makes the first steps towards creating clean water and sewerage services.

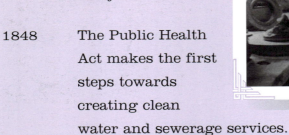

1870	Dr Thomas Barnardo sets up his first home for orphans.

1870	The Education Act gives powers to School Boards to start up schools.

1873	Children under eight years old are banned from working on farms.

1875	The practice of using climbing boys is banned.

1880	The Education Act makes it compulsory for children aged between five and ten to attend school.

1891	The Government makes education free and compulsory for all children.

Ideas for guided reading

Learning objectives: sustain engagement with longer texts, using different techniques to make the text come alive; appraise a text quickly, deciding on its value, quality or usefulness; use the techniques of dialogic talk to explore ideas, topics or issues; improvise using a range of drama strategies and conventions to explore themes such as hopes, fears and desires

Curriculum links: History: What was it like for children living in Victorian Britain?

Interest words: abacus, asthma, Empire, Industrial Revolution, phosphorous, poverty, scullery, sewerage, tuberculosis

Resources: rough time lines from 1800–2010 in ten year stages, whiteboards and pens

Getting started

This book can be read over two or more guided reading sessions.

- Read the text and look at the pictures on the front and back covers of the book. In pairs, ask children to discuss what they know about Victorian times.
- Share children's ideas and focus on what life might have been like for children then. Use the photographs on the front and back covers to prompt discussion.
- List three questions about the Victorian age based on the discussion.
- Draw a rough time line from 1800–2010. Ask children to predict where the Victorian age fits.

Reading and responding

- Look at the contents together and decide which sections might include information about when the Victorian age was.
- Remind children about skimming and scanning strategies. Challenge children to find the exact dates that Queen Victoria reigned and mark them on the time line (p3).